THE
HATCH

BROOKLYN ARTS PRESS | BROOKLYN, NEW YORK

THE
HATCH

JOE FLETCHER

The Hatch
© 2018 Joe Fletcher

ISBN-13: 978-1-936767-54-0

Cover art by Sam Mayle. Edited by Joe Pan.

Published in the United States of America by:
Brooklyn Arts Press
154 N 9th St #1
Brooklyn, NY 11249
www.BrooklynArtsPress.com
info@BrooklynArtsPress.com

Distributed to the trade by Small Press Distribution / SPD
www.spdbooks.org

Library of Congress Cataloging-in-Publication Data

Names: Fletcher, Joe.
Title: The hatch / Joe Fletcher.
Description: First edition. | Brooklyn, NY : Brooklyn Arts Press, 2018.
Identifiers: LCCN 2018002192 (print) | LCCN 2018004568 (ebook) |
ISBN 9781936767564 (ebook) | ISBN 9781936767540 (pbk. : alk. paper)
Subjects: | GSAFD: Horror poetry
Classification: LCC PS3606.L482 (ebook) | LCC PS3606.L482 A6 2018
(print) | DDC 811/.6--dc23
LC record available at https://lccn.loc.gov/2018002192

First Edition
10 9 8 7 6 5 4 3 2 1

CONTENTS

I

Coastal Healing	15
Thousand Hills Radio	17
The Match	20
Kindergarten	22
Umbilicus	23
Rusty Squeezebox	25
Isaiah	26
The Hooked Atom	27
The Colorado	29
Northwest Passage	31
Saturn Day	32
The Vegetable Staticks	34
Otway	36
Okeneechee Racetrack	38
Suite for Henk Boerwinkel	39
Wayne	44

II

Mazurka	48
The Wake	51
Tune	53
Leonora at the Window	55
Ponce de León	56
Flatlander	59
Tomb Trip	61
The Fly	63

Ringing 64
Self Defense 66
The Hatch 69
Transplant 71
Jack Mike 74
The Bird Nester 76
Atchafalaya 78
Palmdale Area 80

III

The Order 85
Thomasina 87
Mediterra 88
The Fiery Trigon 89
Perceforest 90
Hoopoe Balm 93
The Electrical Congress
        in the Mountains 95
Mine Disaster 97
The Breathing Fields 98
Spring Break 101
Memories of the Future 103
Double Transduction 105
The Organ Grinder 106
Muselmann 108
Beksiński 109
The Dalles 111

THE
HATCH

While sleeping, watch.

-Heinrich Khunrath

I

COASTAL HEALING

Why did god give us sexes
if everything is to burn?
I asked the failed suicide.

His jaw was shattered
so he couldn't answer.
He looked toward where
I was through the cloud
that draped his face. His one
working nostril wheezing.

I cleated the jib line.
The sun warmed my back.
A cormorant flung itself
with a healthy violence
into a brown roller.

Out here you could believe
that each thing nursed
a seed of purpose swelling
on the vine of correspondences.
I ate a plum as plum-colored
clouds fused above a piney isle.

Out here I could follow
this fat, mute captain to any
destruction of a destination.
His scarred hand trembled
gently on the tiller.

He knew this about me.
In such a wind he for once
did not want to be
forgotten. Some tobacco
juice dribbled down
his ruined chin
as he tacked us in-
to the thunder.

THOUSAND HILLS RADIO

There was a ship
that droned through the star-pierced night.
In a cavern of glassy rock
men hatched murders.
The empress' child staggered
behind the peacock, transfixed
by the flickering cosmos in its plumage.
Nightlong the sickly sea sludged
against the sagging sea-wall.

No one touched the fly-speckled mangoes
on the banquet table.
Beneath blankets beside the cane-clogged creek
sleeping mouths exhaled their malarial fumes.

You walked with a knife or
you were hunted.
You shared a cabin with strangers
and learned no names.
Something danced through the windy forest.

The general turned his face to a distant chorus
of diesel grind and people shrieking.

We looked to the skies for water.

A rusted crane succumbed to vines,
jaw unclenched, and toward dawn
a paw-shaped cloud loomed above the shore.
A priest twitched in the straw.

A doctor fingered the emerald beads on her bracelet.
A wingless bird pried a nut
from the shadow of a smokestack.
Seven metals smoldered in the mountain's oven.

For all the world's talking, the soil
still threw forth its barbed foliage,
its extravagant blossoms, which dazzled
the passing convoy.

Hornets nested beneath the fountain
gurgling in the embassy garden.
Whose daughter solemnly buried
a rabbit beneath this papaya tree?

The pamphlets said nothing of the stench,
the dust-streaked jeeps descending the ridge,
the soldiers' skin deepened to purple,
their breath of goatmeat and mustard.
We saw what happened to the others, and yet:

Here comes the same sun
over the shanties and tidal flats.
Here comes the president,
so close to the screen you spy the elastic of his wig.
He chews a root that makes his mouth orange.

The insect-clicks of cameras devour him.

Then the clamor of excursions,
a horn blast erupts in the careening marketplace,
buses rumbling through the smoky throat of the city.

The watcher on the ship watches the watcher on the shore.
On the terrace of a shrine a mirror tilts toward the sun.
Our fingers warm with rooster blood,
we climb the day-splashed slopes.
If there is a word that stops us,
no one will say it.

THE MATCH

Nothing in me wanted to wrestle my father.
He'd been training his whole life.
What advantage could I have had, my youth
spent spindle-legged in meadows,
swiping a butterfly net through sunbeams?
My sisters delighted in pranking me,
pretending to see something
in the water off the end of the dock.
When I scampered over and stooped to see,
they pushed me in, laughing.

My father sprinted on his "walks."
He worked in industry, surrounded by
the gnashing teeth of power tools, howling saws,
thick, throbbing machines I cowered from.
As I shuffled to the bathroom after being
put to bed, I heard the clanging barbells
and grunts from the basement.

Was life reducible to power?
I found out in the ring.
I had no idea how old my father was.
He looked vigorous in his shiny red trunks.
I crossed my arms over the moles on my torso.
My sisters pushed me toward him.
All the books I had devoured and where
was the change? We grappled.
He clobbered my face. I bit his shoulder.

He panted threats in my ear,
breath smelling of vinegar.
We lowered ourselves to the mat.
I chased away the serpent
of surrender in me.

My mother clapped in his corner
and would not make eye contact, even
when I screamed her name
as he kneed me in the groin.
Then I looked at father. Really
looked hard for the first time,
entwined as we were:
he was shriveled.
He said "I love you,"
or "surrender,"
his voice faint
as ash flakes
from a cold cookfire
left by a doomed army.

KINDERGARTEN

You pull a child from the earth and stuff five autumns into her.
A blue wind dries an eagle heart in canebrake.

She is not as you dreamt she would be.
On your neck you feel the cool breath of a god.

The unbearable yellow spreads in the locust leaf.
Into the old yellow forest you carry a candle.

In the wildwood you mistake a knot of branches for
the skull of an elf king who haunted your childhood.

You never told her where you prowled, at the pregnant hour
when the dew was forged, when the real's deep joints were carved.

A horse weeps. A black seed, your terror is now hers.
What can your touch, your little nest of gravity, do?

Child, your father has been dragged through eleven cancers.
You watch him eat cold soup before he leaves the earth.

You dig a small grave for a lizard in the side of a hill.
Two stars whisper above. About you.

UMBILICUS

Hunger swirls up in us
like a savage vortex.
Thus it is good to live
in a city so generous
with beefsteaks.

I wander
through dripping forests
of meat trees, branches
hung with red marbled cuts.
In my crisp linen suit
I look like a fang.

You have to wait,
a hot bundle of appetite,
then speak into a speaker.
For a few coins
extends the branch
to release into your hand
the hot flesh fruit,
swollen and oozing
in its paper skin.

Evening: pork sizzles
in a thousand flames.
We pack our guts
with slabs of goat
in the meat district,
which is everywhere.

Who says the glutton
is wrong? Amidst a steak-
eating contest, my friend
cries out: "If you're going up
to the bell, ring it!"
The bell is a ribeye.
We ring its bone with knives.

I'm linked to my loves
by chains of meat, greasy ropes
flossing my innards; I kick
through fly-buzzing rib-racks
and bone splinters cracked
by ravenous jaws, grunting
in delight. We find a rind
of fat someone left behind.
We suck it together, squatting
on the moonlit cobbles.

During meals we discuss prior meals.

I wake, fumbling
for the gravy-soaked loaf
at my bedside. Its density
comforts me like a planet.

RUSTY SQUEEZEBOX

It would have been comical
had not the obscene child in the clown
wig drawn, from a single oboe note,
such swarms of pain—such an immense
birth in the viney shadows of the hills,
such isolation that clamored in need
of an utterly unfulfillable fulfillment.
With the trowel of his chords he sought
to pry some divine secret from the worm-
chewed loam beneath the Viennese
cobbles, and the scandalized continent
sought refuge in the frail light
of its waning polestar. As the arias
percolated up through his lusty
powdered stem, a twin-faced specter
drifted from the chilly mists to reclaim
its errant spark while I and the others
dumped his blighted body into the un-
remembering grave where waited
our sharp old god.

ISAIAH

We found him kneeling
by a stream in the forest,
head submerged, naked ass
to the air. We thought him
praying, and quit our joking
to approach soft and curious.
Close enough to cast a stone
at him when he pulled his head
from the current and whipped it
round to face us, beads of water
flung from his braids. He was
on us, laughing and flicking
our throats. He said he cared not
for consequences, heard the voice
of god like a roach buzzing
in his ear. "You people," he said,
gesturing as to encompass
our entire being, "You worship
blocks of wood!" And dissolved
again into laughter, stretching
the lines of the rhombus tattooed
on his face. He sprung at a pile
of our freshly chopped cedar
and screamed "Save me!" forty-four
times, his contorted lips grazing
the hewn wood. Then raised up,
turned toward us, spat some ash
into his palm and dissolved
into a cloud of words.
I looked down at the thing
appeared in my right hand.
The lie.

THE HOOKED ATOM

I climbed out of a cab in Mumbai
with a throbbing hand
and a mouthful of paste.

Night was a black stone
dropped from a bridge
by a blind child at night.

And then suddenly!
The void allowed revolutions.
A strumpet kissed a clubfoot.

My laughing after a meal
was composed of laughing atoms,
their atomic mouths stuffed with veal.

"Mathematics are a ladder
in the wild," you said, drunk.
"Climb it to reach the real."

In a casino bathroom in Malta
I vomited two red dice
into a woman's hand.

An overconfident child, perched
backwards on a mule, I led
some tourists down a canyon wall.

My mother could not contain me,
I told a man on a sun-cracked boat
in the heat-flattened Chesapeake.

"I am not your father," he said,
turning his irisless eyes toward me.
I stopped laughing.

THE COLORADO

In the canyon the light smelled old.
I removed the aspen leaf
pressed between my forehead and hat brim
and held it, as if expecting a falcon
to descend and pluck it from me.
The others looked up,
their faces glowing jade,
a kind of pain.

We made camp beside the river.
We peeled bean husks from a skillet.
A dog gnawed audibly on the femur
of a steer tumbled down a gully.

The fire accelerated as we added dried mesquite
and a woman transformed there before us.
She stood up, wept to be renamed.
She leaned forward to vomit
the anguish of her prior life, convulsing
the story of an epic in which winds
harnessed from a blind angel's throat
steer a convoy to a shattered coast.

A voice in my tooth woke me.
Embers hissed in the still dark.
I crawled from my tent, through
the dreamwebs of the others,
and kept crawling.
I was about to drink from the river
when something made me look up.

A light had swung around the riverbend.
A lantern.
On a little skiff rocking in the wavelets.
It shed such luminescence I knew
it was not inside my head.
I felt the flame at the root of my tongue.
Before I could call to it
the river carried the lantern beyond me.

NORTHWEST PASSAGE

There was a street in Oregon I was walking down. A thick gray sky saturated my thoughts. I heard a motor increasing. A thick gray van approached. It stopped beside me. Someone had spray-painted a crude neon chickadee on its scraped and battered side.

The driver lowered the tinted window. I saw his thick gray face haphazardly spread with stubble. The window shielded his lips. With his head he gestured me to come closer. I did.

"Can you help me with my baby?" he asked. "Your baby?" I said. "My baby," he said, "Listen." I listened. From within the van, I heard the sound of a baby crying. Shrieking, really, as if it was lying naked and alone on a rain-soaked piece of plywood in the wind-ravaged heights of the Cascade Mountains. It sounded like something was biting it.

Listening like this, my head absently pressed against the window, my mouth making a little oval of steam on the glass. With a gaudy pinky ring, the man tapped the window from his side, startling me out of my attention. "Can you help me with my baby?" he asked again. "It sounds a lot like a recording," I said. The pattern of shrieks repeated every few seconds. His bloodshot eyes indicated that my speculation had offended him.

"Fine, I'll check it out," I said. I walked to the back of the van, opened the door, and climbed in. Someone shut the door behind me. It was dark. In here the crying was louder. There was a lot of it. I caressed the cold knobs and the blinking lights of the recording equipment, making shushing noises.

I thought of my friend, who was coming to visit me from some distance, who now would never find me, accelerating as I was in someone else's direction.

SATURN DAY

The savage tears his shirt off
and shits on the backside of
his mask.

He returns to his birthplace,
reclining for the camera
on a verdant ridge,
munching wild tubers,
wheezing like an ox.

The savage hurls *Émile*
from a speeding convertible,
his blazer stained by a milkshake
a woman in tears threw at him
outside an apartment in which
her sleepless mother watched,
her own memory pried apart
and converted into nothing
by what she called thornworms.

The savage sees money
as a kind of flower he takes
from you with the gentleness
of a medieval novitiate,
the pads of his fingers smooth
as a sturgeon's tongue.

The savage ingests mushrooms
at a rooftop gathering in Cairo
and hours later is beckoned to

by a wooden deity standing
in billboard shadow, smelling
like a crushed star.

The savage tries
to wake us to the absolute,
appealing to what he calls
intuition, naming thereby
the unreason, but thank god
he's outside where we can
watch him.

THE VEGETABLE STATICKS

A form pushes me
into itself from within.
I am the shape
of the sound of a drum.
A smart wind blew
a space open in my head
where I think the blue jay
that tears the shell
from the drowsy beetle
and inhales its sap
would be nothing
without its hunger
but a massless singing.
How could I think that
without the medullary
fibrils, the tegmentums,
meninges, and pons
curled like mushrooms
whose throbbing gills
have drunk magnetic light
of red suns somewhere?
An angel told me this, and
that in infancy a fancy
face floats down through
the forest canopy and
sticks to our blind, bald
raving heads smeared
with tears and snot.
When the tingling roots
find soil, you first see

how little you can do,
how there is no you
without the influx.
"What about you?" I said,
reaching at the angel,
who drenched my hands
in rotting colors and
with a whistle, withdrew.

OTWAY

On the pier, then, I was one with the warm black wind. You couldn't put a candle down anywhere. Nor see the channel.

Waiting. The salted wood creaked. Clouds of insects ravening in the reedy shallows where a child's pink shoe bobbed.

I hung on to my can of beer. The tense rod angled over the railing. The suck and give of tides.

"A cloud at night," you said, your red face tipped back. The cloud, monstrous and silver, slid over the marshland. Two people shouted at each other in a nearby trailer.

My jeans were crusted with shrimp juice. I hung on to a cigarette with my mouth.

Humans writhed in the backseat of a dented sedan behind a kudzu lump along the dirt road. We heard their radio across the waters. We heard them shouting. The dog barking in the distance, the radio towers blinking, the silkworm moth diving toward the gas station glow.

You pointed. A boy wearing a wooden mask stood in a canoe, gliding toward us over the inlet. He was sobbing loudly. I couldn't figure how the vessel was being propelled.

How could we rise to greet him? We didn't. The prow of the canoe collided with the pier. The boy might have fallen into the water, but he didn't.

He climbed onto the pier, his sobs amplified by the mask.

He walked past us, down the pier, to the tangled shoreline. His sobs echoed across the hushed waters.

Something struck my rig with such force the rod leapt. Behind me, a crashing sound erupted from inside the trailer.

OKENEECHEE RACETRACK

In a parked car outside a faucet warehouse
I ate a spider believing it would change me.
A man on the radio called for war.

Sunday sun dove into a nest of pine crowns.
A wet dog passed, trailing a bloody leash.
Panting, I scanned the disused quarry.

My father's father stole from an orchard.
My father stumbled home smelling of the racetrack.
His scarred and hairy forearm above my bed.

That night I took my son's hand.
We walked a woodland trail to the empty bleachers.
We stepped through the broken fence.

An owl lifted from the river's stinking
sluggish rim. No sound as the moon tugged
our inner tides and an insect shifted

in the weathered pressbox. We sat and watched
the overgrown track, a gray band in the dark,
until a switch flipped somewhere and bright bulbs

mounted high on their wooden poles
shocked the forest into a glare. I saw my son
an engine speeding away from me.

SUITE FOR HENK BOERWINKEL

I.
At the edge of autumn
I came to a wall. At night,
with night's insects.
A wall with a square hole in it.
I reached my arm through the hole
and felt it bathed by waves of silt.
I let my arm play in that elsewhere.
It came back to me,
intenser, more coherent.
I looked through the window and
I saw:

II.
A soldier crawling along a trench,
the barrel of his shoulder cannon
pressed to his shaven cheek.
His boots matched the brown clouds.
His shrapnel-dented helmet so low
his eyes weren't helping. Who needs
eyes when a mouth can open like his?
He paused when my gaze touched him.
Shook his head. Then crawled on.
I saw:

III.
A shrouded peasant hoeing a plot of turf.
His broad, coarse turnip face tipped up
to the forest lid as a prey bird screeched.

His hungry torso flickering in his coat.
Who hoes in a greatcoat and a tophat?
He did.
Can you farm mushrooms?
He did.
I saw:

IV.
Floating like the weather, like a mind,
a bald one lit by an offstage moon,
suspended horizontally in the air,
grasping a pole shot up from the loam
and swallowed by clouds.
He stared at me through a strip of gauze
wrapping his eyes and tied behind his head.
Another strip of gauze kept a leaf
pressed over his mouth as if to cover
his sex. He swam away.
I saw:

V.
An unlidded crimson box on the moss.
Two hands grasped the upper edge
from within. Up rose a cat-eyed gnome
with no scalp—just a level plain
above the brow. A bald plane of skin
over the jubilant pineal vault he crawled
from to see what the chorus gave rise to.
I saw:

VI.
A hand reached out of what
I thought was at first an empty well.
Not the first time I was wrong.
This hand was trying to help a druid organize

against disintegration, fear pressed
onto his almond-shaped head, itself pressed
into a conical, tasseled hat.
The hand helped raise the druid's hands
in a trembling gesture of supplication.
A gentle finger-tap to his sternum.
The hand withdrew, and flicked a net
of magnetism into the druid,
who wobbled toward genuflection,
still not knowing what to do with his body.
He ambled toward a magnifying mirror
through which he bent his druid gaze.
The hand created
a suction as it withdrew.
I saw:

VII.
A banshee made of gas and thin hoses.
Its fingers were marsh straws.
It let the wind be its form.
I saw:

VIII.
A red-haired clown slumped
atop a wall beside the monastery.
I watched it notice the strings
extending upward from its hand.
Excited, it climbed them, head tilted up.
From above a hand shoved it back down.
The clown shook. Clutched the strings
again, and pulled itself up until
the hand again denied its ascent.
Up. Shoved down. Up. Shoved down.
The hand grew tired, and grabbed the clown
by the right elbow at the point where

if a god grabs you, you die.
It did.
The hand lifted it limply
into the nether.
I saw:

IX.
An old woman on stilts appear
from behind a stone mill.
She had the stilts to keep a basket,
which was bigger than she was,
which was wicker and strapped to her back,
from dragging in the mud.
She stopped and turned toward me.
The basket was wet and heaving
with the breath of something inside.
I saw:

X.
Three magistrates mutely rocking
in a lifeboat on a churning sea.
Their imminent deaths lent them
a newborn solemnity. They rested
their hands on their craft in such a way
I realized they were blind and
reading events in the wood.
I saw:

XII.
A woman in rags, leaden eyes, hands folded
over the head of her staff, come shuffling.
Her mouth opened and I thought as no one
had talked, surely she wouldn't. But she released
a searing yawp, a yodel dropping into laughter.
Her laugh morphed into a mourning dove's

cooing, then rose to a howl that defied breath,
which revealed her as no woman but a hound,
which in its glee or fury had taken a corner
of the night in its jaws and would not let go.

WAYNE

My neighbor, Wayne, found a dog lurking near the railroad tracks behind the Dexter Mill. Alternatively languid and frenzied, the dog had disemboweled a mourning dove, trotting into the woods as Wayne approached.

Wearing a sweatshirt emblazoned with the logo of the local university, Wayne tailed the dog through the winter evening. He squatted by a creek as an icy moon swung up over the Poconos. The dog lapped at the current twenty-nine yards downstream.

Just before dawn, the dog lay down in meadow indentations where deer had bedded the night before. Wayne, a big man— 6'5" and over 300 pounds—belly-crawled through the snowy field and paused within eight feet of the hound.

Seventeen minutes passed, silent but for the occasional crack and creak in the depths of the winter forest. Constellations twisted in the cosmos. A plane bound for Omaha blinked silently as it split the sky. Wayne's exhalations melted a divot in the snow. The dog began to snore.

Wayne leapt. The dog, nearly crushed by his mass, yelped, squirmed, and gnashed in futility. Wayne's meaty hand clamped the dog's muzzle shut as he sent a series of harsh whispers into its ear. The dog's eyes rolled in terrified comprehension.

Wayne works as a produce supplier for several local grocery stores. In the spirit of holiday cheer, I invited him over a week ago. Though he lives next door, he arrived at my door, framed by the night, like an Inuit chief journeyed down from the ice-clenched tundra. There was a dog pressed against his left shin.

Wayne is prone to big-bellied chuckles. He challenged the structural integrity of my furniture. He got some eggnog on his moustache. His wife died during a boating accident on Lake Erie in 1987. During his visit, he allowed me to take his coat and shoes, but he refused to remove his wool cap.

I played my violin for him, which he did not ask for. We opened a second bottle of cabernet.

After frowning at his watch several times late in the night, he declared that he had better get home. I nodded, dizzy. Embracing him was like being enveloped by a bear.

I was half-reading, half-drifting off when the dog emerged from the back room. Terrified, I dropped my book. The conversation began.

II

MAZURKA

A child on a footbridge in Kansas drops an amulet into a stream. Years later the child is part of an ethnographic expedition in the jungles of Honduras. Fording a muddy stream he plunges his hand into the current and withdraws the same amulet. That night, while urinating beyond the circle of camplight, he is mistaken for a member of the resistance and shot.

A man happens upon his therapist in a grocery store. After calling a pleasant greeting to her, she flies into a rage, berating him for his "masochist passivity."

Sunday afternoon outside Père Lachaise. My sister and I are approached by an elderly man in a maroon blazer. He is bald, sweating, and smells of wine. Seeing that we are studying a map, he offers us assistance, detailing numerous routes to our destination, reverently commenting on the landmarks we might pass. Then he bows deeply and enters the cemetery. We watch him clamber up the slope lined with sycamores, humming to himself like a spectral merrymaker hurrying to a shadow carnival.

Central Prison, Raleigh. Robert DuPree is escorted to the gas chamber. He breaks free and sprints down the corridor, throws the doors open, and leaps into the seat on which he will die, a grin splitting his face.

Two men disembark from a ferryboat in Freetown. As they saunter down the wharf, one man places the first two fingers of his right hand in the second man's mouth. They continue until they reach a restaurant, where they are seated opposite each other at a table overlooking the port. They are served steamed clams. The waiter grabs one and stuffs it into the second man's mouth. Tears stream down the second man's face.

In a chestnut grove a man slaps the face of a horse.

A retired professional football player is found dead in his apartment in Nashville. An officer mistakes a corner cabinet for the girl whose virginity he bragged he took before the war. Later, he tells his wife there are certain cities that are unlucky to see in a dream. Nashville is one.

"It would be foolish not to acknowledge the sexual act implied by a city's towers penetrating the sky," says the theorist. "And we should pay attention to new cities with their ascending architectures, for here we have a virginal act. One can sense the tentative negotiations between tower and sky; the yielding; often entire tracts of sky are revealed in the process, offering their glistening contours to the perspective of the citizen, unleashing rivulets of silence upon the avenues. Depending on the character of the city's architects, who are only ever unwittingly channeling the animus of extension energy at that particular locale, the process can be more violent. Pockets of sky can sometimes be ripped into being prematurely, and if this happens at night, one can be subject to harsh lances of sudden starlight. This happened to me in Dubai..." He continued to speak. I was in the back row, holding a sleeping child. I suddenly had the sensation that the child was not mine.

A woman in the Philippines receives news of the death of American entertainer Michael Jackson moments before she is to see a film. In the dimness of the theater she unleashes sobs into her hands throughout the romantic comedy. Upon exiting, she notices several other people with reddened eyes.

Dusk in Toledo. A man approaches me on the sidewalk. He drains the contents of a can sheathed in a paper sack and tosses the empty into the brush beside him. I veer into a parking lot where my car is, anticipating that he will call to me. He calls to me: "Hey buddy." "Sorry, man, I gotta go," I say, removing my keys. "I just want a motherfucking cigarette," he says. "I don't want any money." I am, after all, smoking a cigarette. I give him one. "I know how it is," he says, as if absolving me of my wretchedness. But he cannot.

THE WAKE

I did not foresee that
the coffin would be too short
and too narrow, like the suit
they stuffed me in, the cravat
digging into my throat.
I inhaled the cloying smell of
varnish and embalming fluids.
They left the lid open, or off.
I might have climbed out
if my hands, folded on my chest,
did not feel heavy as mountains.
After a tedious succession
of heads bending over me
(the children's faces probing,
unblemished by the decorum
of mourning), my gaze restricted,
I sensed myself being
hoisted above the throng
of mourners—so many I
wondered how I could be
the sole cause of this procession.
Above us clouds hissed
across stars which glinted
like lustral water. I saw raised
hands, banners, upper windows
of buildings from which strangers
leaned, shouting. A woman
let fall a handful of yellow petals.
A boy held a cat to his chest,
eyeing me while mouthing

the words to the hymn they sang.
Music blossomed from a band
marching ahead of me and I
heard a man's voice through
a megaphone, sometimes
directing the singing crowd,
sometimes reciting Psalms
in a Hebrew-Spanish hybrid.
A blimp trained its light on us.
The crowd roared as it was
illuminated. On the blimp
was a face. Mine.
I hated that face.
We passed out of the city.
The crowd vanished.
I heard the pallbearers
panting. We entered a tent.
A lantern flickered from a pole.
It had begun to rain.
There was a grinding noise
as I was lowered into the pit.
I could not read my head-
stone as I dropped.
I could not read
the cold earthen walls.
The lantern went out.
At the bottom an eye
cracked open. I felt
a greater wound.
Dark shapes scrambled
towards me.

TUNE

I went looking for the doctor
and found instead his mysterious patient.

An egg caught a current
into the pastures of her brain.

How did an axe get smuggled into the asylum
inside a pair of filthy overalls?

There were suddenly only six gardeners
swinging lanterns through the birches.

Barbed commands hatched
from the egg's inner skies.

She was like certain opera fans
who listen only with their clitorides.

Crushed, glistening vanillas
swallowed by the spore-dusted machine.

If someone pulled the string of winds
that started the bells, she's gone now.

The baroque pool in which the grotto
is doubled has a bloody tint.

I was suddenly covered in tongues,
lashing across the stage like a muscle.

Who was she waiting for beneath
the bouquet of rusted horns?

I was not the one they called out for, but someone
had to be wailing in the eclipsed distances.

Someone had to be pulling a tooth
from the cool forest beneath the forest.

LEONORA AT THE WINDOW

Some houses, pressed against the autumn wilds, lean into the drift of time like shipwrecks. Tonight's wind splits against the corner of one of them, finds an open upper window, and enters to wake Leonora.

She emerges from the window unencumbered, eyes shut, arms fused to her torso by webs of flesh. Her breasts and buttocks do not droop but wobble. She extends upward into the air, her legs joined in a single pale stem.

She undulates, absorbing sidereal transmissions. From her toothless mouth a tongue protrudes. An errant moth veers close. The tongue lunges at it, misses, retracts behind smacking lips.

Across the field, in a sickroom, a candle has been lit and a cough pierces the night. At the sound, Leonora recoils through the window, an anemone sucked back into the interior of a reef.

The first stormdrops strike the face of the nurse as he hurries across the field. Below her window he pauses. Streamers of silver mucus hang from the clematis. The flowers burn his hands as he collects them.

PONCE DE LEÓN

I.
Florida dawn: pink clouds reflected
in marshes where egrets prowl,
bellies slogged with flounder.
His army wades through the muck,
encumbered with useless bronze,
cannons abandoned to the blazing shoals.
Their eyes are bleary from sleepless nights
strafed by insect swarms and
the shrieks of marauding skunk apes
which they mistake for the screams
of those they massacred.

II.
The sun carves them,
their reddened faces swollen like mangoes,
their reed-stuffed talismans clenched
as they navigate a cypress grove.
In a basket they find, wrapped in cloth,
a cow tongue under white corn
and rotten eggs in a clay bowl.
When the cloth is unfolded,
his name appears smeared inside,
with three Spanish coins.
He believes he is made of glass and
stares helplessly into weather
while water is drizzled to his blistered lips.
Only after being fed bean sprouts
does he sit up and call for his maps.

III.
His plans ferment.
His letters to Havana are intercepted
by boatmen draped in alligator skins,
who slit the throats of couriers
leaving the bodies to be shredded by garfish.
Scouts stagger back to camp raving about
a green-skinned girl who scratched
at the flaps of their tents.

IV.
He listens. He thinks
the land sprouts from a single spring.
He fingers his jade ring
while his men sip squid milk on the sand.
They harvest salt and carry pouches inland
to trade with farmers for peppers
they roast with cock sparrows
on platforms beside irrigation trenches.
Orange-winged birds drift in from the gulf.

V.
After months of circuitous forays,
dwindling rations,
raids by local tribes, he flings his breast-
plate to the swamp and demands
to be carried on a pallet,
half-naked, clutching a musket.
He orders his men to submerge their heads
in crystal rivers, scanning the bottom
for vents to the underworld.
The native guides grumble,
thigh deep in a mangrove lagoon.

He signals their exccution by raising
his left eyebrow.

VI.
In Bimini he wanders off alone at dusk.
Rustling seagrass meadows sound to him
like the gurgling fountain. He gluts on
what he thinks are rejuvenating freshets.

VII.
Children spit on the coffin
carrying his poisoned corpse
through the streets of San Juan.

FLATLANDER

He trudged along the canal. The skies were empty and hot and smelled of paint. Four towers pierced them. One had blinking red lights. He tried to find a pattern and couldn't. The tower was of tinted glass cubes that shimmered. How far was it from him? There was a sloppy tangle of forest between them, broken by construction sites where men's faces could be glimpsed through the scratched plexiglass of bulldozer cockpits. Birds flickered through the branches and wires.

He passed fishermen on the banks, beside their fishless buckets, cane poles clasped between their knees. Their faces were furrowed from weather. When he asked they gave no help or direction, yet he liked to get close to them and their grandfatherly scent, to peer into their hairy ears and glimpse in the gloom the bunched spindles of line unspooling as their sinkers sank through the muddy depths.

Another tower was an unclimbable smokestack of copper that belched a stinging smog. His head felt like a target. He looked around. A pack of dusty hounds clawed a bag in a weed-choked lot.

The third tower had water in its oblong head. The water was carried down in pipes that snaked underground and was rumored to emerge through the crawlspace spigots of ramshackle millhouses. At night, sleepless on his square of cardboard, scratching his reddened skin, he heard their dripping. But by day, despite his searching, his canteen swung empty from his belt. He stayed by the canal, tried to drink from it once but vomited.

The fourth he saw only once. He had found a goat that wasps had killed and he cooked it over a fire of splintered railway ties. He scraped the flesh from the hide with a spoon. What he didn't eat he tossed into the canal. When the water smoothed he saw the tower in its surface. It was sandstone, tapered to a point so fine he couldn't tell where the tower ended and the sky began. He bent to look closer. The tower shattered as four carp thrashed over the goat remains.

TOMB TRIP

We packed a light lunch of figs and cornbread.
To contain our meditations, our driver forbade us to open
      the windows.
I looked out at the sun-dazzled hills.
Shirtless men with chainsaws were diminishing an acacia grove.
They did not sweat in the dry air.
I got restless and started to sing. The others reluctantly joined in.
The driver did not.
He wore sunglasses over his regular glasses.
He chewed a spicy Persian leaf.

The tomb was a cave carved into the very rock.
The driver reached out and gave some money to a man just
      standing in the dust.
The man wore a frayed brown robe, perhaps a uniform.
We drove right into the cave.
The cave curved back into a darkness probed by our headlights.
I wish the driver had driven more slowly.
I glimpsed vivid paintings on the vaulted walls.
In one, a winged serpent coiled around the reaching arm of
      a drowning sailor.
Another depicted a laughing satyr cradled in the roots of an
      upside-down tree.

I don't know how long it took to reach the rear of the cave.
It ended as if its creator suddenly had something else to do.
Just a rough stone wall.
We idled ten yards from it.
On the cave floor was illuminated something that looked like
      a jackal turd.

"Is that a jackal turd?" I asked the translator, who asked the
     driver in another language.
I wondered why the driver kept his sunglasses on.
The driver said something to the translator, who turned back
     toward me.
"It's a cocoon," he said.
I shut up and waited.

THE FLY

Summer found me
and friends in a boat
with a laughing baby.

We smoked and drank
and sang, speeding
through our sunburns.

Jenny spilled Campari
on Jordan's chest.
Life glistened.

Then I pried a dead fly
from the thoughtless
baby's hand. I took

a breath and thought:
If not for me the baby
would've eaten the thing.

Its wing still quivered,
as if trying to speak
from beyond life.

I ripped the wing off
and held it to the sun.
An impulse made me

turn to what my friends
shouted after: the baby
bobbing in our wake.

RINGING

After the death of my brother's tutor, a great astrologer who drowned himself in a pond near Montpellier, I heard less and less from my brother, despite my frequent and perhaps over-anxious missives. I was told by my mother, swollen and sagging with dropsy, that he was living with a soprano, with whom he had purchased an abandoned beet farm.

In July a deep purple weariness penetrated my head. I found myself in bed until midday, a film of sweat coating my brow, the papers on my desk greened by a layer of breeze-borne pollen that had infiltrated the open windows of my study, outside of which raucous jays plucked slugs from the garden walks. A cruel sun swerved, uncoupled from its elliptic, over distant forest fires, which I could smell. My pack of pornographic playing cards, the concertos of Liszt, failed to rouse my viscous attention. "I will find my brother," I said one evening to my slumbering cat, and reached into the bedside drawer for my knife with the garnet-encrusted hilt, once grasped by a marquis.

I set out at night. The moon glazed some deer sleeping so close to the road I could have prodded them with a lance. They did not move as I passed, barefoot, snacking on a handful of thistle. By evening the next day my gout was inflamed. I stole a willow-wood crutch from a maid who let me climb into her room on the second night.

Does travel enrich one? Yes and no. Did it wake me up? No. I dreamt that I drifted up to a statue of the Baron d'Holbach beneath a riverside willow. It bled from its nose. Galaxies swiveled in the waterfunnels spun from my willow-wood oar.

On the fifth day, I bent my path from the thoroughfare and plunged through a furze meadow. I found my brother within hours. Our father—who is in heaven—had always said that conception had dropped a kind of magnet in each of our heads, around which the breezes spun our reciprocal fleshes.

My brother was in an extreme position. It took my eyes some time to believe it. Some crows flapped away from picking at him as I approached for a better look. Was he alive? Yes and no. He had been crushed by a massive bell engraved with shapes that shifted as I moved. Its top was black and smooth. It had made a pit in the earth, and from beneath its weighty lip my brother's head and some mangled limbs protruded. His mouth was open and some cables snaked out, far across the meadow, into a treeline, beyond which rose a white windmill, its three blades ponderously spooling the air. His eyes were open and I stepped into his gaze. "Now," I said, and it was true.

SELF DEFENSE

I.
I saw a woman
with four wires
extending
from her cheek
into the fog
engulfing the gingko
she stood under.
I was a young shepherd.
"Open your eyes wider, "
she said. I don't know how
she said it. She said,
"There is a fence in you."
The fog thickened.

II.
I was thawing my body fireside
when a wolf approached and spoke:
Do not alarm yourselves.
I am the King of Ossory.
I was alone.
It looked at my white thorn staff.
With its claw it inscribed
on the flesh of my arm
two concentric circles.
I woke up at the edge
of a frozen lake.
The wound never healed.

III.
I came upon two men
loading sticks into a horseless cart.
Giggling erupted from a nearby path.
I asked for directions. The men responded
as if I were two women, far from home.
They pointed to me. To my destination.
I came to a kiosk in the woods beyond which
the path split.
There a man sat hunched.
One hand protruded from a sleeve
and produced from the other a brass doorknob,
which he gripped tightly, his body clenched
in the effort to open it.

IV.
I followed the path to a courtyard and joined a crowd around a languid sow. They hosed it and scrubbed it and trimmed its whiskers. Around its neck they fastened a purple cape with the words *noli mi tangere.*

We entered a courtroom. The crowd was frenzied. The sow was led down the aisle. One tried to attack the sow, but was restrained by a red-bearded man. All were silenced when a gun was fired upward.

The councilors for the defense were pleased. The sow simply lay on a crate. Once, the magistrate leaned over and spat on its snout. It grunted and rolled its eyes. It followed the proceedings with its idiot gaze, finally falling into a slumber when the village children were called to the stand, declaiming and shaking fists at the defendant. A court guard nudged it awake before the judge read the verdict.

The crowd erupted. The sow was placed in a cage on wheels and pulled into the courtyard. The crowd was a chanting semicircle around a stake, sharp end upward. The sow, bewildered but calm, was led up some steps and lowered onto the stake tip by the executioner. A flock of tomtits were startled from a distant hedge.

THE HATCH

It was late. A student was walking home. The frost had melted and daffodils nodded wearily beside a bicycle chained to a parking meter. The garden wall curved behind the seminary, its windows glowing faintly, as if a candle guttered somewhere within. It was too early in the season for insects; the student's thoughts pulsed in time to the scuff of his boot heels on the walkway. Through a gap in a hedge he glimpsed a housing development. Blue television flicker reflected off lacquered siding. Nothing stirred on the serpentine drives. A peal of laughter broke from an open garage, which sounded to the student like a recording.

He walked on, his shoulder chafing against his bookbag's strap. He wished for a donkey he could load with his burden and swat lazily with a switch. On a wire extending from the roof of a vacant laundromat, a bird widened its eye at his passage. A traffic light yellowed and reddened and bobbed slightly in a breeze.

A man hunched on a bus stop bench. Did the buses run this late? The moon slid behind a highrise. The air held an echo of warmth. Fish stirred anxiously in industrial ponds. As the student passed the man, he heard a voice: "You have any change? I'm—" "Sorry," the student said and hurried away, his shoulders curled chestward defensively. A generator churned to life in a concrete lot behind a medical supply warehouse.

The walkway led to a park. The student ran his fingers along a chain-link backstop. He crossed a footbridge spanning a dry sewage runoff strewn with crushed cans and shredded plastic snagged in the rhododendrons. The smell of skunk cabbage drifted down a slope thick with massive oaks. He could no longer see his hands. He whistled. A whistling answered him. He stopped and shined his penlight on the moist earth.

The whistling continued. He lifted a patch of leaves and found a human head shorn of hair buried up to its chin. Its eyes rolled toward him and it began to pant. The head was swollen and shiny with sweat. Mucus ran from its nostrils to its thick upper lip. The student squatted beside the head. "Do you need help?" he asked. The head swore and spat. The student unscrewed his water bottle and dumped some on the head, which sputtered and cursed and tried to twist away.

The student clamped the penlight between his teeth and dug at the soil with his hands. The head continued to curse, and when the student brought his hand close to the mouth, the head snapped at it. Soon a trench had formed around the head's base. But as the student dug he was surprised to find no shoulders—just worms and potato beetles. The head was bursting with hatred. The student scraped toward where the neck should have been, but there was no neck.

He persisted. Soon the head was supported only by a narrow column of soil, which crumbled and collapsed beneath the head's thrashing. The head toppled into the trench like a balloon filled with mud. It lay there, face upwards, glaring at the student.

The student noticed a pink cord extending from the bottom of the head into the earth. To what did it connect? He touched it. It felt like a whirlpool. It felt like many whirlpools tunneling through him. The head's eyes rolled back. Wind rushed among trees. The penlight fell to the earth and went dark.

TRANSPLANT

On the day I lost my leg
my family and I were walking
among the Indian Snake Mounds of Ohio,
having descended miles from the lake
where pale children floundered
among the waveless shallows
and purple storms coalesced
over the western deeps.

My daughter found a saber in the dunes,
where we lunched silently on crackers
and peppered salami, watching gulls
scuttle on the roofs of broken bathhouses.

My sister carried a sleeping baby
upside down inside her.
I was trying to approach my wife
gently with my thoughts.
She was turned within
to cares I could not see.
My son was watching, writhing
with the cloud of restlessness
he swallowed at birth.

A family is always preparing
for a change it only notices
after it has happened.
My family held hands
before the valley and the rains.

The forest was so fragrant,
the river so richly brown
and swollen that we laughed
to be living. Swallowtails
darted along the mapled banks.

A man approached
selling jars of honeysuckle nectar
and we bought one.
Another man stared
at our passage from beside
a guardrail that long ago
had crumpled aside at a truck
careening to the sumac-
choked ravine below.
Green slopes exhaled
drifting tendrils of steam.

The sun stung my father's eyes.
He rode atop the packmule,
fed through a tube in his chest,
and declined our fireside games
but sometimes woke us at night
with a joke or aphorism
that left us confused, nervous.

On the night before the day
I lost my leg
I awoke
to a yellow grasshopper
which leapt thrice
over my prostrate limb.
Its wings snapped.

My father awoke
and gazed into the embers.
"A worm is drinking
among my teeth,"
he said. I dropped
back into a dream.

When I awoke
my left leg was disappearing.
It was blurred and tingled.
I rubbed it. My brother
rubbed it. All morning
I limped south with them.
At lunch we stared at it.
By afternoon I had to be helped.
By evening I sat down.
I told everyone to be calm,
which calmed me.
So many years preparing
for my leg to be
torn from my torso
and now this effervescent
dissolution, like a mist
thinned to nothing.
I laughed and opened my eyes
to the faces above me.

This is how I walk.

JACK MIKE

I'd operated on him the night
before, after two too many brandies,
in a tent behind the dancehall
under a bulb swinging in the fake
breeze of an oscillating fan,
his wife holding his bare scabbed
ankles, eyes shut to his moans.
We all looked up when the storm
started pelting our makeshift station.
I held aloft the dripping stitching needle.

"Not too bad," I whispered
as the drugs pulled him unresisting
from the raft of consciousness.
His wife and I walked
into the thunder-riven night.

Early that morning we dressed
him in his torn pilot's garb
and moved him before he woke
to a hammock beneath an elm.

Later he sat up with a shout and bounded
into the dewy meadow. Chickens
grunted in the dirt outside the barn,
and we watched him try to get there.
Some flicker in his head drove him askew.
He stumbled in a furrow and ended up
on his side, his legs still acting
like they were walking.

How could he have seen—
with the skin sewn over what were
his eyes—the sow come staggering?
We watched its hooves crush his abdomen.

He kind of lived for a while,
harnessed to motorized pumps.
Until one of his daughters,
sleepwalking, tripped over the cord.

THE BIRD NESTER

He ambles through the markets,
his chest stretching his tunic.
Holds forth at taverns
with a slovenly bravado,
encircled by an attentive band
of millers and wheelwrights.
What color are his legs?
They are always covered
by brown woolen leggings.
His ruddy hands bear the scratches
of twigs, and he likes to place them
on the passing busboy's bottom.
He smells like willow.

When spring rolls over the misty banks
of the Rhone, he ambles through the landscape
like a burly woodchuck. If you see the crown
of a poplar shaking amidst its still neighbors,
he is in it. If you hear snapping branches
within a hedge, he is getting what he is
after. He carries a cone of sanded birch—
nearly as tall as him. He is not tall.
He aims it at the copse he is about to enter.
A mellow trill emits from it, and the mother
birds fly out, twittering helplessly.

In a field once, he and I watched wrens
swarming a crow. Trying to escape,
the crow swept close to us.
My companion sprung into the air,

and grabbed the bird,
which appeared larger
once taken from the sky.
He stroked its black breast.
The wrens scattered.
The crow gazed into his eyes.
Something was communicated.
He released it.
It circled once, squawked, and departed.
On the walk home he wordlessly
showed me the black egg.

ATCHAFALAYA

In the South you see
a honeysuckle-scented man
strangled on the seagull-
studded slope of the landfill.
Two children grab a heel
and drag him away, noon
measured by the shadow absent
at the base of the nearby steeple.

A truant officer protected
from sunburn by a blond beard
strokes his black plaster
Christ replica as Squeaky's
vendor cart, full of pink shrimp
spread upon beds of chopped ice,
rattles past on the frontage road.
Squeaky draws his trade
behind his bicycle, muttering
a Creole hymn in the green
shade of his visor.

In the chicken processing plant
a fermented specter
weaves through the ordure-
pungent coops as the steel forklift
blades scald the palm of the worker.

When the president tours
the provinces he sits in a closed
Norfolk Southern freight car,

throwing dice with crouching
migrants by torchlight,
a Dixieland swing bursting from
speakers on the peach caboose.

If you leave a word hanging
in the air too long at dusk
it sprouts obscene tubers
twining toward unintended
connotations, and you are
pegged as a foreigner,
and the locals deny you
their gaze and so you roam
beneath a sweaty moon
with a crotch rash and a head
torn by the bronze shrapnel
of bourbon. But there are
mothers working down here
with breasts as wide as deltas
and sometimes they tangle
you in embraces, their breath
smelling of chicory and
reptile, nodding in time
with the riverside chorus
of insects and the more
distant surfbreak
of the creeping,
radiant ocean.

PALMDALE AREA

A salesman flings keys from a pier.
A toddler sleeps on the sticky floor among popcorn buckets at
    the cineplex.
A clicking is heard from the scrapyard.
A satellite is reflected in the hotel pool.
A cook fondles himself at a bus stop.
Bacteria spread in waves through the bowels of a shrimp.
An addict's parents, over a bottle of Tempranillo, nurture the
    vacancy between them.
An orchestra eats yellow food from paper bags on a lawn.
A vagrant beneath a bridge swipes at the shadows with a
    windshield wiper.

A wailing ambulance screeches to a halt in the driveway of 135
Mimosa Lane. Paramedics force their way inside. No one home.
The dishwasher is running. One paramedic finds a book entitled
The Choice of Valentines in the arms of a doll in an upstairs room.

The mute boy carries a bucket of orange paint through the marina
    at dawn.
The kidnapper breakfasts alone in the atrium.
A cell phone tower marks the intersection of three skies.
A monkey whispers to a monkey in red laboratory light.
An electrode plunges for answers in meat.
Hornets pry the head from a caterpillar on the asphalt outside
    the bank.
A man shouts at his child after driving beneath power cables.
A parrot chokes on an almond in a botanical garden.

A flight attendant vacuums her own earing in the aisle of a deboarded plane. The jetway retracts with a whir before the attendant can exit. She sits in first-class, fingering her earlobe, looking over the tarmac to the nuclear plant smokestack on the far side of the fake lake where a man was electrocuted to death while swimming during a storm.

A grandmother speaks into a monitor.
Ants infest a rain-soaked pizza box in the strip mall parking lot.
Gloved fingers brush debris from the skeleton of a camel.
Wrestlers grapple on a grid of television screens in a darkened
      appliance store.
An arrow points at itself.

III

THE ORDER

Because I have a fear
of hunchbacks, a hunchback
was my waiter. He sat across
the table from me, his chin
resting on his hands. No menu.
After watching me for minutes,
he said: "I'll have the viper heart
stew and a glass of five penis wine."
I said: "I'll have the viper heart
stew and a glass of five penis wine."
"Yes sir!" he said, smiling and
bowing. He shuffled to the kitchen
through a beaded curtain. I swooned.
A tap on the shoulder woke me.
My waiter handed me a cloth sack.
"Go get them yourself!" he said.
"But—" I began. "Go get them
yourself!" he said, pointing to a
side door. I exited with the sack
into a dirt yard with a flowering
tree in its center. In the yard: a dog,
a sheep, a deer, and a bull; two
vipers were twined in the tree
branches. The four mammals
were easy—I slid underneath each
and gave a little tug. They winced,
but did not struggle, perhaps
relieved to be relieved
of the burden of their virility.
I stuffed their members in the sack.

How do you find a snake penis?
You let the snake coil around
your head and press its sex
to your eye. I did this. There was
a pair of tweezers in the sack,
which I employed. I felt stronger.
I sang in the ear of the viper.
It jerked three times, its jaw
opened and its heart popped
into my open palm, like a frog
leaping from a cave opening.
Into the sack it went.
Into the restaurant I went. Into
the waiter's hand went the sack.
Into the kitchen went the waiter.
I heard sizzling through the curtain,
which parted as my meal was
delivered. My mouth parted as
I devoured it, sending the spoon
clattering in the empty bowl.
I kissed my waiter in gratitude.
I tipped him and departed,
parting the teeming throng
like the prow of a ship
carrying a newborn caliph.

THOMASINA

Her expansion stopped long ago.
Draped in silks, she fills her tiny sphere.
A bundled microcosm bouncing
in the corner of a royal carriage
on the pocked road to Mortlake.

Rain gleams on the asparagus fields.
A breathless hilldigger clenches his spade.
A bucket of tripe steams by the riverside
where a fish eight times her height once
lay bloody and gasping on the bank.

A little breath bounces in her little neck.
A big cold current swings through
the river elbow. When she asks for food
it is not very often, and in Italian.
Laughing, they lower a meal to her.

She is lowered to the walkway
by gloved hands the size of her torso.
A Tuscan amulet presses coldly
to her breast. She drinks in the scent
of horse dung and eggshells bubbling

in stills, wafting from the buildings
on the hill. One small foot at a time,
Thomasina. You move in the golden
nets of the queen's love. And here
comes a green meteor to anoint you.

MEDITERRA

You slow down. Your body drinks
more light. You let May come.

A dry throb where desire was.
Rubble of pines. Tar gash.

Women go forth in search of berries
tucked among the dew shade makes.

You strap a child to you and see
how you do. You are a circle.

Spirits orbit a temple a bride sleeps
within. The sheep bleat.

The Aegean is as deep as Pluto's
finger. He stirs intelligences.

A golden oil you coat your words
with. A speech remnant in bark.

Did we not convene in this starry
village to forge a dream?

To stroke the orchard's underside?
You cannot keep the hill-climb burn.

Laughter from a boat moored
in a turquoise, meteor-carved cove.

My love, you do not have to move
me. The mountain's door opens.

THE FIERY TRIGON

What appears? What lowers
a milky and sky-wide eye
to the nether end of Brahe's scope?
What blind tuber twines from
shadows born in the eclipse?
We stroll through a garden
of dark rays, and stoop to peer
into the glinting veins forking
through steeps of Canadian ice.
We eat rice with sawdust
soaked in hen blood and acorns
spilled during the quake that tangled
the four directions on Iberian flats.
My two children leap as if tomorrows
will continue to unspool from
the creaking loom behind the moon.
My two children sleep as if the meteor
was an arcing ember faintly tracing
the scratched smoked glass of night.
I lie awake in the frosted grass.
Some sick man stutters a poem
about ships splintered against
the sea-frothed fangs of rock.
The sailors sank to seabed graves.
But something in the sky saves us,
makes us look more closely,
or for a last time.

PERCEFOREST

I.
I broke my mechanism
and then wanted it back.
I was carried along the clearcut
below power lines to an office park
around whose pesticided fringes
the forest percolated.

II.
I was not the only one needing to be
put together, as the ragged caravans
from across the seaboard attested,
sunburned women scarred by wars,
eyeing each other vacantly
across atomized hotel lobbies
while their husbands ordered steaks
to be carried by stoned adolescents
from the back rooms of chain restaurants
on plates mounded with starch.

III.
Some numb clouds were packed inside
a capsule inside a New Jersey complex
and helicoptered down to us. We washed
them inside us with cola and flipped through
glossy gun magazines which pictured
barrel-chested men organizing landscapes
by pointing a scope at them. We waited.

IV.
When the staticky fog began to wash
away the scaffold of my sensorium
I looked once more out the window
and through the humid foliage saw
six stags strung from their hindquarters
and dripping thick ochre from their throats.

V.
How did I get inside the humming room
where I was undammed by a thick-
fingered doctor who called herself
Danielle, her inhale denting the cloth mask
covering her entire face, which I saw when
I surfaced like a carp from the muddy depths?
How did she get inside me?

VI.
From behind her mask and from below
the lamp the mute assistant
held for her, Danielle said hers
was the vision around which
my life was aligning. She clapped
to wake me and to congratulate
herself on the work well done
and endless.

VII.
I emerged with a system
I could articulate in its entirety
from the inside. I am told I did this,
exuberantly, even as I could not walk,
even as I was pushed in a wheeled chair,
swollen and bleeding, across the tiled atrium.

VIII.

I thought a stranger was pushing me
until I smelled Danielle's cologne
and I relaxed into the chair as she steered
me across the vacant nighttime parking lot,
across the strip of mowed lawn between
some fireflies, into a row of sumac, the
crimson torches of their seed cones dripping
through the revolving forest. I felt
Danielle's big arms working in the dark.

IX.

We came to a languid river on which
a glowing shuttle idled. Before I boarded
she embraced me, which is all healing is.
She breathed into the whirlpool of my ear:
You are reversed.

HOOPOE BALM

The roots of hoopoe balm twist through skeletons of spice convoys buried in the Tyrolean peninsulas. Its blossom is the color of jaguar blood, and when a breeze springs from the tropics it scintillates like champagne at the feast of the Queen of Sheba. In its fragrance mingle coreopsis and jasmine, with an acrid undertone, like the spit of a tubercular child. The petals are rubbed to the lips of epileptics. In the notebooks of Hippocrates, one finds hoopoe balm designated as *Artemisia hydrastis*, indicating its origin as a hybrid of wormwood and goldenseal. Robert Fludd concocted a tincture from crushed stamens for the purpose of dissolving saltpeter. Carthaginian soldiers placed leaves of the plant beneath their helmets and, sweating in the desert, received visions of crystal palaces built on sun-gilded cirrocumulus.

In midsummer children plunge their arms into vats of its nectar, chasing through gardens flocks of butterflies pausing from their migration to sip from fallen hoopoe fruit. The traveler, dusted with pollen, glimpses the moon strangled by its clambering tendrils. During the Siberian solstice, buds exhibit negative heliotropicity, burrowing beneath the tundra crust while the pink roots burst like bouquets of vipers toward the sun. Sealskin traders kneel in the shade of their root canopies.

In the year of the Plague the tributaries were clogged with stalks of dead hoopoe balm. The waters were acidic and the riverboat pilots manned their vessels with bloodshot eyes. From the crushed fields rose the drone of beetles that had decimated the population. Those that touched a drooping leaf or stood in a pollinating wind later fell victim to rashes that coiled about the neck. It's what killed Don Carlos of Ecuador. Black bells were installed in the temples and a stinking phosphorescent moss crept over the balustrades of pavilions. Women dreamt of giving birth to dead catfish and rain-wet dogs gorged themselves on the corpses of antelope that had grazed in the hoopoe meadows. But after the famine and the rains and the echoes of war, a small tuber shot forth, this time from Indonesian sands...

In the Mesopotamian basin, after the last fruits have been plucked, fires are lit from the dried stems and leaves. Barefoot farmers prepare the fields for the next crop in the dew-sprinkled hours before dawn, when the winds have retreated to their caverns behind the stars. And the infant, wide-eyed in his cradle, hears the rim of the world slicing through the ether.

THE ELECTRICAL CONGRESS
IN THE MOUNTAINS

was held in a humming cave
on a slope of quaking aspen
where men once roamed
to gather wood for us,
dragging axes behind them.

We stuffed dirt in our nostrils
to facilitate concentration
on the speaker, who was
projected to us from a glass-
walled Bolivian highrise.

"There is money in the sun,"
I remember him saying.
I remember brushing the thigh
of the one beside me.
I remember a spark.

It was so dark in there I now
cannot read my notes.
Was that the point?
I suck on a lozenge I took
from a bowl on the way out.

It tastes like rain and sap.
I look back up at the towers,
the blinking mountain
looks down at me.
Electricity is still

missing an explanation,
which allows it to work.
I am shocked to find
the lozenge is shaped like
a light bulb disappearing.

MINE DISASTER

A child does not want to interpret her own drawing of a butterfly on fire and backpedals across the moss.

The elderly Greek couple see their silver heads from above, retroactively positing themselves from the grave, waving from the deck of a cruise ship the narwhal intuits via an extended electromagnetic sensorium.

A supermarket contains a back room accessible by tilting a wooden leper. Inside, the aisles are lined with mason jars filled with tar and containing fossilized zoophytes from a time before time was given.

Love! Like a cardinal exuberating in the May shade of a linden. A cardinal who lets a madman gently smear honey on its belly.

"Sea oats sprout from any pocket of existence," says a daughter of mine, a disaster, who rolls her eyes at her own formulation and returns to a nebulized existence flanked by tidal currents, while I become pregnant with a misgiving.

My sister brings an oregano sprig indoors from a Parisian balcony, cradling it in her palm as if she is carrying a baby plucked from the sooty throat of a mine shaft. A sexless baby that moves like a kind of water, an insect, a flower.

THE BREATHING FIELDS

The counter-tenor on the trestle.
The correlational vacuum.
The yellow-helmeted workers wading in the delta.
The ambiguous armistice.
The seeds of plague on the wind.
The humid path, or
The discourse on the vegetable menstruum of Saturn.
The slow winnowing by a mercury-scented lakeshore.
The soldier's bloody vomit beside the fountain.
The twisted cloud.
The river of minerals beneath the river of water.
The woman running her hands over a cedar stump.
The coral blastula.
The crabapple sores.
The invalid's brooch.
The crimson creeping across October.
The crisp wine that enhanced your view of the waterfall.
The deposed dictator sobbing on the radio.
The train that took my sister away.
The astral voices from which we learned of medicine.
The deaf surgeon.
The foundry lights slurred by rain.
The homunculus whose beard smelled like salmon.
The sketch of the villa inside the violin case.
The view from the summit of further summits.
The woman beside the turnpike who had no left eye.
The woman beside the turnpike who pointed at you as you passed.
The portrait of Otto X.
The murder in the Catskills.
The silent lunch.

The bark tincture that the shaman spat on the scar of a
        kneeling camel.
The dolphin carcasses swept through the offshore wind farm.
The diplomat's fantasy.
The aphid's choice.
The letter to Trithemius slipped into the apprentice's robe.
The boy who threw acorns at the mailman.
The mailman smitten by palsy.
The finch bone lodged between slimed river rocks.
The blanket in which the dead dog was carried to the crematorium
        was the same blanket with which Joanna covered her breasts.
The yawn that tore through my mother's head, and mine.
The falcon performing idleness for the webcam.
The dripping, lemon-scented forest you ran through.
The demon accidentally summoned from the Pleroma.
The bicameral breakdown insinuated by cocaine.
The drowned bodies beneath Winnipeg ice.
The hoax.
The monastery blanketed in night noise.
The physician who devoted himself to the nervous system.
The worm that burrowed in you to flee the tropics.
The waterlogged pamphlets dredged from the schooner's bilge.
The bloodthirsty roar of the stadium crowd.
The tire bundles slung down a chipped pier wall.
The smoke-stained grain they fed the infant Pascal.
The clanging behind the barn.
The triangles loosening in the bone.
The oiled tusk your uncle gave you.
The baby whose fontanel I pressed with a thumb.
The fire that cut my hand.
The comet streaking the pupil of the beached perch.
The saint gesturing atop the cupola.
The needle ejaculating into the purple river of a vein.

The unsatisfactory explanation.
The crest of the dam from which the lovers slipped.
The child wandering through the parking lot.
The tree inside which spring silently opened.
The candle wax dried to a page of Pliny.
The faceless archers.
The drunk bishop sneezing against a bus window.
The crown over which two brothers grapple on the scalded dunes
       of an island nation.
The one-winged titmouse that trusted me.
The building in which we grew up.
The vacant building.
The reach.

SPRING BREAK

I went down to the bayou to check my crawfish traps. I wore tight green shorts and a tight green shirt. My sunburned arms were swinging beside me. I had my stick and my bucket. I did not want to be anywhere else. Hornets droned above humid patches of clover. Billions of fire ants screamed through the epidermis of the earth. I stepped out onto the ramshackle dock that jutted into the brown water. Egrets croaked in the rustling rushes along the bank. I knelt down and with my stick I lifted the trap and watched with racing heart the netted bottom swinging up from the depths, the pale hunk of bait meat clipped to its center. Vague forms were scrambling to flee the ascending contraption. Some of them succeeded. But not all. I shook the trap above the bucket and a few crawfish flopped into it and twitched and snapped their shiny bullet bodies. One clung to the meat and I had to pry it off with my bare fingers. "We're going to eat you," I informed it, before dropping it in with the others. I lowered the bucket lip to catch some warm river water so they wouldn't die until we wanted them to.

I noticed some loose mud on the bank. More crawfish? I knelt down again and began to dig with my fingers. No crawfish. Just a shallow hole. Something made me lower my ear to it. I got to my knees. I heard a voice say: "The doctor walked around in the nowhere until she was tired. Whereupon she rubbed her breast until the earthy grease spurted from it. From it she shaped a soundless spheroid. With her lone finger she poked four holes for each direction, all of which oriented the nowhere to stream into that clod. 'You are here,' she said, and coaxed hair to grow around the holes. The hairs were crimson, as if tinged from a fire in the center of the clod, where nervules twine into a bolus the doctor called *The Auditorium*. The cartilage shafts of each hole need daily to be wiped clean of the gum that accrues when matter reacts with eggs in the air. That is why your hands were made."

I broke away from the voice. My bucket heavier with my sad knowledge, I went looking for the next trap.

MEMORIES OF THE FUTURE

When the mother
lifts her veil, a flap of skin
falls open and the wound
greedily sucks the air.
She could have stopped this
with her eyes,
and does.

I was there.
We will have a good time.
Josianne spills brandy on the piano
as laughter rolls
over the terrace and lawn
and into the dense municipal woods
where a speckled egg
trembles in a nest of needles.
I stare hard and can
see inside it.

"Wait for your eyes," she says.
Then a bubble in her neck will begin
speaking behind her voice,
like the pigeon-toed porter
behind the lantern he was and is now
carrying through Little India
with a head not yet blasted
by smallpox.

I'm no technologist, so
had she told me her arm was real,

I will have never known.
It's warm and nuanced and
when I touched it I feel orbits.

At dusk among virgins
at a waterfall I lit a match
and I'm told to come
back tomorrow.
"You said that last time,"
I will say, parting their ablutions
to drink up constellations
shimmering on the river.

Nothing will have lasted forever
is my philosophy.
I can write it for you with an ember
if we're close.
I could carve it in coral
with my mouth.
I will call it rivering
and quiver to have thought it.

The mother makes an example
of me, saying she can't give me
tomorrow. Did I believe her?
Today will come
pressing against the inside
of my face, pushing me
into a when.

DOUBLE TRANSDUCTION

Grandmother, crooked in her wheelchair,
admires me trimming the juniper,
some conditioned procedure my arm
executes without needing a me to tell it to.
She is along for the ride, and for this
she thanks in silence the ragged Nazarene
who at death questioned his own besouledness.
But who was the questioner? asks a voice
from the left inside of her head, where I
once as a tear-watered seed took root.
The wrinkle nest of her face
gashes into a smile of lipstick.

Grandmother asks mother who my parents
are. This is the end of any grandmother
I might save in a drawer. Here is a kind
of withered flesh funnel. She was kind,
you might say, but to what might you
truly point? She sorts her purse contents,
gasping at what squints back from the make-up
mirror she arthritically fumbles open.
The neural web of fibers, done vegetating,
done emitting a self, unplugs, lifts from
the brittle skull and wafts to the porch
ceiling, where it flutters like a kerchief
thrown by a soldier from a train.

THE ORGAN GRINDER

Love loves to wander.
Time made us so.
Should I join you,
circling in the snow?
A little paper blows
along the ashen gutter.
A chimney hides
a shriveled sun.
Near death, your hands
bleed easy. Already
your feet, numb,
are in the black lake
rising. Some music
does not know how
to be alone. Yours
knew nothing else,
rolling back to signal
even the cold wastes
were not infinite.
I heard you laugh
once into your death
pillow I think it was
a laugh there was
a lamp at least you
left on the ice-clung
fence around which
night foliated immense
oily leaves. Window-
side awake again I
hear a brook gallop

through an ever-re-
mote May, smell
faint linden fruit in
frozen hay, o do not
say what I think
you know even as I
lean toward the silent
singing of the piano.

MUSELMANN

I did not mean to collide with you
to graze your ear with my withered lips
for I am a cube for you to dump
your hatred in then violently avoid
for I am an infinity of voids
spilling at you through trainsmoke

listen if I spoke I did not mean to
so unlisten to me strange stranger
so far away from you I blossom like
a filthy cherry in your entrails
unfurling my brute algorithm
in the musty cellarage the bloody syrups

thank god there is no subject
just a fleet of traumas orbiting organs
entangled like a bolus of watersnakes
when you bayonetted me it was like
stabbing a pillow which bled a little
I did not mean to I am the I who

slips out of meaning take no care of me
I took a cockroach that did not try to flee
into the star-hung night you could
not say there was nothing there
you could bayonet me my neighbor
to give my life meaning to love it

BEKSIŃSKI

Beneath the starry shell a writhing knot of knuckles was born.

They stitched the dead monk's lips to keep Jehovah's breath out.

You could not infer a pineal eye from the given two, and yet…

The cathedral contained St. Anthony's shredded tunic in a
    glass box.

Man chased the sun. Webs of bat bones collapse to dust.

The Pharisees say otherworlders killed the savior and carried
    his heart across ice. The bloody trail was watched from
    within a windowless hut.

A flatbed truck loaded with sleeping child soldiers rattled past
    the makeshift derricks.

Lichen embraced the sagging villa. You lifted a square of eel meat
    to your face.

The mariner entered the wedding and exhaled the toxic mist into
    the groom's ear.

You let a dog guide you across the plains. You both slept beneath
    a patch of carpet you tore from a shuttered hotel lobby.

The titan's shape was visible beneath the waves. You could not hear
    the fire.

I watched your lips move against the gauze. Something was
      inside the piano.

You kissed the earth and knew for a moment how it saw you.

In the jungle a helmet, in the helmet a spider, in the radio, fog.

The cloud was illumined from within. You turned away. Grew old.

A wind flattened the trees. The fiber circuits were appeared to.

Your caretaker's son murdered you, which was only a rearrangement
      of matter.

THE DALLES

In the Dalles a man was killed with a seven-pound steel bolt.
Five river gulls descended through dusk.
They have a wind there that smells of basalt.
A boy dipped his hand in the puddle beside the sawmill.

In the Dalles no one tells them not to carry knives,
so they do. They sell a milk there that tastes
like a fungus grown on the underside of the moon.
The officers wear slouch hats.

In the Dalles they're all about to laugh at the sick joke
you're thinking but won't say.
I saw butterflies mating on a flaking hydrant.
I saw a child sleeping beneath a parked car.

In the Dalles, if you walk through diesel fumes too slowly
the slurring wretches will stagger to you
and paw your crevices for coins.
Some goddamned person stole the manhole covers.

In the Dalles I met a hazel-eyed miner.
But there are no mines in the Dalles.
I don't know the rules there but I wanted to
stay bathed in the industrial lights.

In the Dalles if you drive a boat fast enough
you can get to night. Some kid's
mother is drunk. Her face is scorched.
She slumps behind the wheel of a grocery truck.

In the Dalles if you feel like you're being watched,
you are. I once sat in a theater there and watched
a girl, painted orange and stuck with feathers,
chase a clipped wren across a torchlit stage.

In the Dalles I fell asleep (I shouldn't have)
on the stained concrete slab of the disused gas station
and I don't know if I dreamt the hands
that groped me in the windless night.

In the Dalles the river resembles a river
on Neptune, and the fish pulled
into rust-blossoming dinghies glimmer
as if infused with the rays of long-vanished stars.

In the Dalles insects carve the green air of evening.
I heard, from behind the surgeon's house,
the rhythmic springing of a trampoline.
I stood there until a dog barked me away.

In the Dalles railyard, graffitied freight cars
languish among the weeds. In their vacuous steel
innards: drifts of rodent pellets illuminated
by the match of a sweating fugitive.

In the Dalles I saw a bare swollen breast emerge
into the naked air from the folds of a floral gown.
Toward it a baby craned its gaping head,
like a bald, blind bird. I leapt with joy.

In the Dalles I had a dream in a motel room—
beneath a giant blue sign with a red number six—
a dream in which I watched a wolf
tear the skin from my brother's neck.

In the Dalles, in my dream, my brother watched
me with the compassion one finds in the painted
saints of Flemish masters. And I watched,
peeling a fruit that smelled of bad meat.

In the Dalles a man wanders the library
flinging impetuous gestures at the patrons.
A radio station plays only organ music.
I saw a bloody towel on the supermarket floor.

In the Dalles a man holding a pool stick said:
"In the Dalles, if you don't like the weather,
wait five minutes; if you still don't like it,
get the fuck out."

In the Dalles that man then opened his mouth
to laugh, and I saw his wooden teeth.
I asked him where his real teeth went.
He said he slept with his mouth open.

In the *Dalles Sentinel* the next day
over a plate of brains and eggs
I read that a man had plunged a pool stick
into the eye of another man.

In the Dalles I have heard at night
the clamor of crowds. But through my motel
window I never see a goddamned thing.
I hear a mechanical thud from the sewer.

In the Dalles there is nothing left
of the judge's house on Monroe Street
but the chimney. The chimney
is cold, crusted, and leaning.

In the Dalles I saw a veiled woman
ascend the steps of the orphanage,
hoisting a writhing sack. Evening comes
early to the unkempt ballfields.

In the Dalles it's evening a lot.
That's when I go down to the docks
and watch the spectral ships pass far out.
I wonder at the dark and distant freight.

ACKNOWLEDGEMENTS

Thanks to the editors of the journals in which versions of the following poems have appeared:

Apartment: "The Fiery Trigon," "The Vegetable Staticks"
The Bakery: "Tune"
Hoboeye: "Atchafalaya," "Flatlander," "Hoopoe Balm"
Incessant Pipe: "The Dalles"
Independent Weekly: "Thousand Hills Radio"
La Petite Zine: "Coastal Healing"
Lute & Drum: "Mazurka," "Saturn Day," "Beksiński," "Perceforest"
Route 9: "Otway," "Mine Disaster"
So & So: "Umbilicus," "Memories of the Future"

THE AUTHOR

JOE FLETCHER is the author of two chapbooks of poetry: *Already It Is Dusk* (Brooklyn Arts Press) and *Sleigh Ride* (Factory Hollow Press). Other work can be found in *jubilat*, *Octopus*, *Slope*, *Puerto Del Sol*, *Gulf Coast*, *Painted Bride Quarterly*, and online at joefletcherpoetry.com. He teaches literature and writing at the University of North Carolina and in the North Carolina prison system, and he is the Managing Editor of the William Blake Archive.

Various, *Brooklyn Poets Anthology*
Various, *Infinite Record: Archive, Memory, Performance,*
    Eds. Maria Magdalena Schwaegermann &
    Karmenlara Ely
Various, *Responsive Listening: Theater Training for*
    Contemporary Spaces, Eds. Camilla Eeg-Tverbakk
    & Karmenlara Ely
Wendy Xu, *Naturalism*

Made in the USA
Columbia, SC
25 April 2018